bubblefacts...

ANCIENT ROME

Miles Kelly
PUBLISHING

First published in 2004 by
Miles Kelly Publishing Ltd
Bardfield Centre, Great Bardfield, Essex, CM7 4SL

Copyright © Miles Kelly Publishing Ltd 2004

2 4 6 8 10 9 7 5 3 1

Publishing Director:
Anne Marshall

Senior Editor:
Belinda Gallagher

Editorial Assistant:
Lisa Clayden

Designer:
Debbie Meekcoms

Cartoons:
Mark Davis

Production:
Estela Godoy

ISBN 1–84236–391–3

Printed in China

Library of Congress Cataloging–in–Publication Data
is on file at the Library of Congress.

Indexer: Jane Parker

www.mileskelly.net
info@mileskelly.net

Contents

 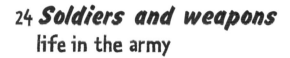   

At home in Rome

city of smells!

Rome was a dirty, stuffy place to live. Poorer people lived in blocks of flats called *insulae* and the smell must have been awful in summer! Rich people owned country homes called villas and during summer they often escaped to them to get away from the smell and heat of the city.

People living in *insulae* threw their waste into the street. The smell would have been unbearable!

Only the rich could afford country villas. They would leave the dirty, smelly city behind in summer.

Villas had central heating. Air was warmed by a wood furnace under the floor, kept burning by slaves.

Father knows best...
happy families

A Roman father ruled the roost!
Each family was headed by a man. He was known as the *paterfamilias* (father of a family). The house and its contents belonged to him and he had the right to punish any family members who misbehaved. Even his mother and other older female relatives had to obey him.

Roman familes included everyone living and working in one household—even slaves!

Lupercalia was Valentine's Day in Rome. Boys picked a girl's name from a hat, and she was their girlfriend for the year!

Roman families liked to keep pets. Statues and paintings show many children playing with their pets. Dogs, cats, and even doves were popular. Some families also kept ornamental fish and tame deer.

Girls married at 12 years of age and most marriages were arranged—love was not considered important.

Roman boys learned to speak well. Schools taught reading, math and public speaking. Boys usually became politicians, army leaders, or government officials and they all had to make speeches in public, explaining their plans. Boys went to school at seven years old and left at age 16.

DOESN'T HE GO ON.

TRIP UP THE WAITER!

WHAT'S THE BEST WAY TO SEE FLYING SAUCERS?

Wealthy students sometimes went to Greece to be taught public speaking by the best Greek teachers.

Students wrote on wooden tablets coated with wax. Others scratched their writing on bits of pottery.

Romans read standing up from scrolls. Scrolls were 33 ft (10 m) long.

The Romans liked a good bargain.

Prices were not fixed so people would haggle until they had agreed on a deal. Markets were popular and sold fish, meat, fruit, and vegetables. Roman shopping was very noisy and streets were often filled with people shouting out their wares!

Roman shoppers had to get up early. Many shops and market-stalls closed at noon.

The world's first shopping center was in Rome! Trajan's Forum was built on Quirinal Hill in the center of Rome. It had more than 150 shops together with a main shopping hall.

Shoppers walked a long way to make purchases because goods were sold in different parts of the city.

Wining and dining
fabulous food

HE REALLY NEEDS TO CUT DOWN!

Romans ate very little during the day. They had bread and water for breakfast and the main meal of the day was around 4 p.m. Only the rich could afford to employ a chef with slaves to help him in the kitchen. Ordinary people went to *popinae* (cheap eating houses) for their main meal, or bought snacks from roadside fast-food stalls.

WE'LL PAY EXTRA— WE'RE STARVING!

WE'RE SOLD OUT!

KEBAB IN MY SHOE...

Fast-food stalls were popular and hot snacks of pastries stuffed with spicy meats sold very quickly!

At parties, Romans ate lying down on couches around a table. The Romans enjoyed spicy food, and food with sweet and sour flavors.

Dinner came in three courses, with a main course of meat and fish. Food was served with lots of wine!

Bathing

Roman style!

The Romans went to the public baths to relax. Baths were more than just a place to get clean. Visitors could take part in sports such as wrestling, have a massage, or a haircut. They could buy scented oils, read a book, eat a snack, or admire works of art in the sculpture gallery!

TAPS, THAT'S WHAT WE NEED.

JUST A TRIM I SAID!

HEE! HEE! HA! HAAA! HAA!

OWW!

WHACK! THUMP! CLUMP!

Bathers went into a hot, dry room where a slave removed dirt from their skin or gave them a massage.

Although the Romans liked bathing, they only visited the baths about once in every nine days!

The Romans didn't use soap to get clean. They covered their skin in olive oil, which was then scraped off with a *strigil*—a scraper made of wood, bone, or metal. The olive oil was kept in a small flask.

THE SAUNA ROOM'S A BIT HOT TODAY!

TRY THE JACUZZI, IT'S GREAT!

YIPPEEEEE!

SPLASH!

NOOO!

To cool off, bathers went for a swim in a lukewarm pool. Finally, they jumped into a bracing cold pool!

Dressed to kill

togas and sandals

Romans wore different clothes depending on how important they were. Ordinary people wore plain white togas made from rough material. Government leaders wore white togas with a purple trim. Rich people's robes were made of smooth, fine-quality wool and silk.

I NEED A TAILORED TOGA!

ONE... MORE... LITTLE TUG...

AAAAAGGGH!

Wearing a toga wasn't easy. It had many folds and drapes and was worn like a sheet around the body.

The emperor wore an all-purple toga—a sign of his importance. Moving in a toga was quite difficult!

Most Romans wore lace-up sandals with open toes. Boots with nail-studded soles were also popular.

Looking good!

top beauty tips

The Romans liked pale, smooth skin. Women used stick-on patches of cloth called *splenia* to cover spots, and they also wore lots of make-up. Crushed chalk or white lead was used as face-powder, red ocher (crumbly earth) for blusher, plant juices for lipstick, and wood ash or powdered antimony (a silvery metal) for eye-liner.

Rich women spent a lot of time and money having their hair styled. Most styles were curled or plaited.

It could take up to three slaves to style one woman's hair! Hair was curled using heated tongs and often put up in a bun. Pins made of ivory or bone kept it in place. Plaited styles were fashionable too. Sometimes women had the cut hair of blonde or red-headed slaves made into wigs.

Women weren't the only ones to be interested in fashion and beauty. Men liked to look good too! They also used *splenia*, small strips of cloth made from leather, used to hide spots and scars. Some men wore make-up and perfume too.

WE CAN'T PERFORM MIRACLES!

SNIP SNIP!

LONG HAIR'S BACK IN FASHION...

COWARD!

While women wore make-up, men had their hair cut at the barbers with long, sharp shears. Ouch!

Center of an empire

magnificent Rome

Rome was a beautiful city.

The main forum, shown here, was a large, open courtyard, used as a market-place. It was surrounded by buildings such as the Colosseum and government offices and law courts. People often came here to meet friends and listen to open-air speeches.

The basilica was similar to a town hall. It was here that people came together for meetings and the building was often used as a court of law. After the rise of Christianity, many basilicas were used as churches.

Market trader

From a small village of wooden huts, Rome grew to be the finest city the world had ever seen.

The Colosseum

Temple

Basilica (town hall)

The Forum

More than one million people lived in this exciting place. The Romans went on to conquer a huge empire.

Place your bets!

chariots of fire!

DOWN A BIT, LADS.

The Romans loved a day at the races. Chariot racing was held at race tracks called circuses. The most famous was the Circus Maximus, which had seating for 250,000 spectators! Twelve chariots took part in a race, each speeding around a 5 mi (8 km) long track. Up to 24 races were held in a day.

WE'RE IN A FOR A BIT OF A BUMPY RIDE!

LET'S LOSE THIS IDIOT ON THE NEXT BEND!

BOING! BOING! BOING!

Chariots often collided and overturned. Many horses and charioteers were killed on the track.

Racing rivalries sometimes caused riots! Races were organized into four separate teams. Charioteers wore tunics in their team's colors—red, blue, white, or green—and each team had a keen and violent group of fans.

The life of a chariot driver was very glamorous but often short-lived as the sport was so dangerous. The best drivers were idolized by their supporters.

COME ON! MOVE IT, YOU PAIR OF OLD NAGS!

NAGS! WHAT A CHEEK! WE'RE THOROUGHBREDS!

CHEATS! STOP THE RACE! THIS IS **SABOTAGE!**

Chariots were pulled by two or four horses. Sometimes six or eight were used for added excitement.

Soldiers and weapons

life in the army

Roman soldiers were well paid and well cared for. Soldiers were given thorough training in battle skills and troops carried three main weapons—javelins, swords, and daggers. Each soldier bought his own set and he looked after them carefully—one day his life might depend on them.

New soldiers trained hard. They practiced fencing and javelin-throwing as well as swimming every day.

Roman soldiers guarding the northern frontiers of Britain kept warm by wearing woolen trousers, like underpants, under their tunics!

Soldiers were given a uniform when they joined the army. Extra clothing or equipment after this had to be paid for out of their wages. They carried shields made of wood and leather and sharp-tipped javelins. Metal helmets protected their heads and chain-mail armor was worn over their bodies.

THAT HURT!

CUP CAKES TODAY, BOYS.

LIGHT AS A FEATHER!

NO, I DON'T THINK IT'S **THAT** BAD.

BANG! BANG!

Soldiers learned to do everything for themselves—cooking, building and first-aid, as well as fighting!

Work, work, work
slaving away

Not all people in Rome were equal. Slaves had no rights and they couldn't vote. They belonged to their owners just like dogs or horses. Slaves were bought and sold at markets. They couldn't leave their owners or choose what work to do.

WELL ROME WASN'T BUILT IN A DAY!

I'M GROWING MY HAIR!

YEAH, ME TOO!

SNIP! SNIP!

YOU CHANGE HIM! IT'S YOUR TURN!

WAH! WAH!

YOU KNOW DIRTY DIAPERS MAKE ME SICK.

Slaves did everything their owners told them to, from cleaning to babysitting to laboring on farms.

Slaves were sometimes freed as a reward for their loyalty. Some sick or dying owners did this so that their slaves didn't go to a new owner who might treat them badly.

From 73BC to 71BC a slave called Spartacus led a revolt. He ran away to a hideout where 90,000 other slaves joined him.

THANKS FOR YOUR HELP.

WHOOSH!

IT'S BEEN A PLEASURE.

Some freed slaves did very well and set up their own businesses. A few became doctors or chefs.

Worship
Roman style
good gods!

The Romans worshiped many different gods. Families gave offerings of food and wine to their gods every day. These were left beside statues inside temples. Some gods were asked to curse people's enemies. Messages were written on metal or pottery and left at temples in the hope that the gods might read them.

Can you believe it?

Livers of sacrificed animals were examined by priests. If diseased, bad luck was on the way!

I SAID SINK!

YOU'RE SO MASTERFUL!

Diana was goddess of the Moon, Neptune was god of the sea, and Venus was goddess of love.

Diana also guarded wild animals, while Minerva was goddess of war—along with Mars, god of war.

Jupiter, king of the gods, protected Roman lands. His wife, Juno, was worshiped by married women.

Roman know-how

clever clogs!

The Romans were amazing architects.

They invented concrete, and discovered how baked clay bricks were stronger than unbaked ones. They found out how to use arches to strengthen walls and designed massive domes for buildings that were too big to be roofed with wooden beams.

Can you believe it?

The word "plumber" comes from the Latin word for lead, used by the Romans to make pipes!

The Romans believed witchcraft caused illness. Doctors could sew cuts and join broken bones.

Water was carried into Rome through channels and pipes called aqueducts. Most of these pipes were underground, but some were supported on high arches in bridges. The aqueducts gently sloped to make sure there was a steady supply of water. The water came from fresh streams and springs.

Roman builders were highly skilled. They used tools crafted by local metalworkers and carpenters, and materials such as wood and stone were also locally supplied. There are lots of examples of their work still standing in Rome today.

WHAT'S EASY ABOUT THIS?

IT'S ABOUT TO GET WET DOWN THERE!

SPLISH SPLASH SPLOSH!

HEE! HEE!

Aqueducts were pipes set into bridges. They supplied the city with fresh water—for all that bathing!

Index